ISRAEL

BY LIZ SONNEBORN

Essential Library
An Imprint of Abdo Publishing
abdobooks.com

ABDOBOOKS.COM
Published by Abdo Publishing, a division of ABDO, PO Box 398166, Minneapolis, Minnesota 55439.

Printed in the United States of America, North Mankato, Minnesota.
102022
012023

Cover Photos: Jek Li/Shutterstock Images (Yafo); Garik Prost/Shutterstock Images (pattern)
Interior Photos: Stock Studio Aerials/Shutterstock Images, 4–5; Spiroview Inc./Shutterstock Images, 7; Vander Wolf Images/Shutterstock Images, 9; Shutterstock Images, 12, 19, 36, 53, 58, 61, 66, 84, 90–91, 101; Mikhail Berman/Shutterstock Images, 14–15; Peter Hermes Furian/Shutterstock Images, 17 (Israel); Web Tools/Shutterstock Images, 17 (globe); Opachevsky Irina/Shutterstock Images, 18, 26; Leo Spek/Shutterstock Images, 21; Imagine Stock/Shutterstock Images, 23; Idan Ben Haim/Shutterstock Images, 24–25; John Theodor/Shutterstock Images, 28–29; Robert Pickett/Papilio/Alamy, 30; Protasov An/Shutterstock Images, 31; Yael Grinberg/Shutterstock Images, 32; Menahem Kahana/AFP/Getty Images, 34–35; Universal History Archive/Universal Images Group/Getty Images, 38, 43; AP Images, 40, 72; Patrick Robert/Corbis/Sygma/Getty Images, 45; Michael Reynolds/Getty Images News/Getty Images, 48; Alexey Stiop/Shutterstock Images, 50–51; Dan Balilty/AP Images, 56; Noam Galai/Getty Images Entertainment/Getty Images, 62; Alexei Logvinovich/Shutterstock Images, 63; Oded Balilty/AP Images, 65; Corinna Kern/Picture Alliance/dpa/AP Images, 67; Roman Yanushevsky/Shutterstock Images, 68–69; Sebastian Scheiner/AP Images, 70; Tsafrir Abayov/AP Images, 74, 99; Seth Aronstam/Shutterstock Images, 77; Jack Guez/AFP/Getty Images, 79; Bettmann/Getty Images, 80–81; Leonard Zhukovsky/Shutterstock Images, 83; Polyanska Lyubov/Shuterstock Images, 85; Davidi Vardi/Shutterstock Images, 89

Editor: Arnold Ringstad
Series Designer: Maggie Villaume

Library of Congress Control Number: 2022940379

PUBLISHER'S CATALOGING-IN-PUBLICATION DATA
Names: Sonneborn, Liz, author.
Title: Israel / by Liz Sonneborn
Description: Minneapolis, Minnesota: Abdo Publishing, 2023 | Series: Essential Library of Countries | Includes online resources and index.
Identifiers: ISBN 9781532199431 (lib. bdg.) | ISBN 9781098274634 (ebook)
Subjects: LCSH: Israel--Juvenile literature. | Middle East--Juvenile literature. | Asia--Juvenile literature. | Israel--History--Juvenile literature. | Geography--Juvenile literature.
Classification: DDC 956.94--dc23

CONTENTS

CHAPTER **ONE**

A TOUR OF ISRAEL

As soon as Rachel's family reaches the hotel, her mom tells her it's time they all go to bed. Tomorrow's going to be a long day. Even though it's almost midnight, 13-year-old Rachel is too excited to sleep. Just hours earlier, she and her parents landed in Tel Aviv, Israel, after spending a week in Greece. Rachel loved lying in the sun by the sea. But this part of the trip is what she's been looking forward to the most. She will get to see Israel for the first time, and she will also be able to visit her grandmother. Nana had lived most of her life in Chicago, Illinois, Rachel's hometown. Yet when Nana moved to Israel a few years ago, she told Rachel it felt like coming home.

The beaches of Tel Aviv are a major draw for tourists within Israel and around the world, with more than eight million annual visitors.

The next morning, Rachel and her parents are up early. At the hotel, they have a traditional Israeli breakfast of eggs, bread, and a sampling of spreads and cheeses before heading out on their adventures. They take a bus across the center of Israel to the city of Jerusalem. Rachel has heard about Jerusalem all her life. She and her parents are Jewish. Like other followers of Judaism, they consider Jerusalem a holy city.

They soon arrive at Jerusalem's city center, where Nana lives in one of its many modern high-rise buildings. Her apartment is comfortable, but it is small enough that Rachel will have to sleep on the couch. After they greet and hug one another, Nana reminds them of her plan. On Rachel's first day in Israel, Nana wants some time alone with Rachel to show her granddaughter around the city.

EXPLORING THE OLD CITY

Rachel and Nana set out for the Old City, a walled area within modern Jerusalem. It is made up of four sections—the Jewish Quarter, the Muslim Quarter, the Christian Quarter, and the Armenian Quarter. Rachel knows that Israel considers Jerusalem its capital city. But her parents explained to her that

TEL AVIV

Located on the shore of the Mediterranean Sea, Tel Aviv is Israel's most cosmopolitan city. It is the nation's economic powerhouse and an important center of the high-tech industry. Its bustling restaurants and nightclubs attract young professionals on the rise. In 1950, Tel Aviv merged with Yafo (also called Jaffa), an old port city with a large Arab population. Yafo is known for its Shuk Hapishpeshim, a vast flea market that turns into a vibrant nightlife spot after the sun goes down.

Jerusalem's Old City features narrow alleys between old stone buildings.

not everyone else does. The Palestinian Arabs there also consider Jerusalem important to them and hope one day to make it the capital of their own Palestinian state.

As Nana leads the way through the narrow cobblestone streets, Rachel begins to feel a little overwhelmed. There is so much to see, hear, and smell. The streets are thick with people, and Rachel catches snippets of their speech. She hears Hebrew, Arabic, and even occasionally English and what she thinks might be Russian. Street vendors add to the chaos, loudly selling their wares, including spices and cardamom-flavored coffee, which fills the air with a sweet aroma. Rachel thinks about how beautiful the city looks as sunshine hits the cream-colored limestone

Arabs make up about 38 percent of the population of Jerusalem.[2]

exteriors of the buildings, making them look as if they're glowing.

Nana expertly navigates through the crowds to reach their first stop, the Western Wall. The wall is at the site of the First Temple and the Second Temple, which were holy to the Jews of ancient times. The Second Temple was destroyed by the Romans in 70 CE. Built 2,000 years ago, the Western Wall was not part of either temple. It was a retaining wall for the great plaza known as the Temple Mount. In the absence of the temple, the Jews consider the wall that surrounded the temple an important sacred site.

There are two areas for the crowd at the Western Wall, one for men and one for women. Rachel watches people pray before the wall. Some people stuff small pieces of paper into its cracks. Nana explains that they have written prayers and pleas to God on the paper scraps.

On the Temple Mount is a large building with a black dome. It is the Al-Aqsa Mosque, an Islamic house of worship. It reminds Rachel that this site is also holy to Muslims. Another structure on the Temple Mount is the Dome of the Rock, which was built in the 600s CE. This Islamic shrine features an enormous golden dome with a diameter of about 65 feet (20 m).[1] The dome encloses a great sacred rock. Muslims believe that the prophet Muhammad ascended from the rock to heaven, where he encountered God. Nana tells Rachel that the rock is also important to Jews. Many believe it is the Foundation Stone, on which God created the world.

The area around the Western Wall features some of the holiest sites in Judaism and Islam.

A BUSTLING MARKETPLACE

When Nana decides it's time for lunch, she knows just where to go. They backtrack through winding streets to the city center until they reach the Machane Yehuda Market. This huge open-air market has operated for more than 100 years. Everywhere there are stalls overflowing with fruits, vegetables, meats, spices, baked goods, and flowers. The market is loud and bustling. Merchants are shouting about their wares to the crowd, trying to attract customers to their stalls. Customers are adding to the noise as they haggle with the vendors to get a better price. Nana tells Rachel the market is even livelier at night, when DJs play dance music.

Finally, they arrive at Nana's favorite restaurant. They eat savory pies topped with cheese and fried eggs. Nana explains that this is not a traditional Israeli dish. The cook is a Jewish man from the nation of Georgia who, like Nana, immigrated to Israel. Nana says that's one of her favorite things about the country. Israel is home to Jewish immigrants from around the world. Nana likes to discover the customs, traditions, and foods that they bring with them from their home countries.

THE JERUSALEM FESTIVAL OF LIGHT

Every summer, the limestone of the Old City turns an array of colors during the Jerusalem Festival of Light. During the event, artists from around the world set up light installations in this historic area. Some project videos onto landmark walls or play sounds to accompany the visual display. This mix of modern technology and ancient architecture attracts hundreds of thousands of visitors a year.

HEZEKIAH'S TUNNEL

A favorite attraction for tourists in Jerusalem is Hezekiah's Tunnel. Its origins are recounted in the Bible. In the 700s BCE, Assyrian armies threatened the fortified city. But its water supply, the Gihon Spring, was outside the city walls. To have access to the water while staying safe from the Assyrians, King Hezekiah ordered two teams of men to dig a 1,749-foot (533 m) tunnel.[4] If visitors to Jerusalem do not mind wading through waist-high water, they can tour this ancient engineering marvel.

TAKING IN ISRAELI HISTORY

After lunch, Rachel and her grandmother take a short bus ride to the Israel Museum. The museum includes many buildings and galleries full of ancient and modern art. It's way too much to see in a single afternoon. But Nana wants to show Rachel a few things in particular. They enter a building called the Shrine of the Book. On display are the famous Dead Sea Scrolls. These are fragments of ancient manuscripts that were discovered between 1947 and 1956 in 11 caves in what is now Israel. The fragments were stored in jars, and the shape of the jars inspired the Shrine of the Book's distinctive architecture. Many of the fragments include portions of the Hebrew Bible, the holy book of the Jews.

They also view the model of Jerusalem. Measuring about 10,764 square feet (1,000 sq m), this scale model shows the city of Jerusalem as it appeared in 66 CE, before the destruction of the Second Temple.[3] Rachel is struck by how different the model looks from the vibrant, modern city she's been touring all day.

The huge model of Jerusalem shows the ancient city in fine detail.

By late afternoon, both Rachel and Nana are feeling tired. They take an outdoor table at a café to rest their feet and have a refreshing *limonana*, a popular summer drink made from lemonade flavored with mint. They talk about all the things they plan to do and see over the next few days. Nana's looking forward to taking a trip to the seaside resort town of Elat. As an animal lover, Rachel can't wait to go to the Biblical Zoo, which houses animals from many species mentioned in the Bible.

Nana is quiet for a moment. Then she leans toward Rachel and in a low voice reminds her granddaughter that there is one thing they must do that won't be any fun at all. They will have to visit Yad Vashem. It is a museum that tells the story of the Holocaust, the mass murder of nearly six million Jews during World War II (1939–1945).[5] The visit will be sad and upsetting, but Nana tells her it's important to help her understand Israel. After all, Israel was founded as a homeland for the Jewish people after that genocide. Rachel nods her head. In just one day, she's begun to understand why her grandmother is so drawn to this special place. She now wants to learn everything about it, both the joyful and the sad.

PAST AND FUTURE

In just a few hours, Rachel discovered some of the many ways Israel is a land of contradictions. It is a relatively new country, having been founded in 1948. But it is also a land with a long history, dating back to ancient times. Historic sites and medieval architecture constantly remind residents of the nation's storied past.

Israel is the only country in the world in which Jewish people are a majority of the population. But the country's people are far from homogeneous. Israeli Jews come from all corners of the globe. Many are immigrants who bring to Israel the customs and beliefs of the countries they came from, sometimes causing conflict. Sometimes resentments simmer between Israeli Jews of different backgrounds, as they also do between religious and secular Jews. Far more fraught is the relationship between Israel's Jewish and Arab populations. Throughout the modern nation's existence, this tension has often exploded into terrorism and violence.

From its earliest days, Israel has been plagued with large problems that have sometimes threatened its very existence. The country has often been at war with its Arab neighbors, and its borders remain in dispute. Establishing a lasting peace is one of the many challenges facing this complex modern nation.

CHAPTER **TWO**

GEOGRAPHY

Many Israelis refer to their country as *Ha'aretz*, a Hebrew word meaning "The Land." The land of this small country includes many different terrains. Within an area of 8,470 square miles (21,937 sq km), there are valleys, plains, mountains, seashores, and deserts.[1]

Israel is located in southwestern Asia in the region known as the Middle East. The Mediterranean Sea lies at its western boundary. It borders Lebanon to the north, Syria to the northeast, Jordan to the east and southeast, and Egypt to the southwest. Israel also shares a border with the Gaza Strip, an area of land on the Mediterranean under Palestinian control. The West Bank, a region on Israel's eastern border, has been occupied by the Israeli military since 1967.

Among Israel's varied landscapes are regions of fertile farmland.

The Palestinian people and much of the international community say that this occupation violates international law. Israel says that its presence in the West Bank is important for self-defense.

Israel measures about 290 miles (467 km) from its northernmost point to its southernmost tip.[2] It takes about nine hours to drive its length.[3] It is relatively narrow, with only about 85 miles (137 km) separating its western and eastern borders.[4] A car trip from the Mediterranean in the west to the Dead Sea in the east takes only approximately 90 minutes.[5]

FOUR GEOGRAPHICAL ZONES

Israel's varied topography can be separated into four different zones. In the northern half of the country, three of these zones are arranged like vertical strips running north to south. The western strip is the coastal plain. The center strip is Galilee. The eastern strip is the Rift Valley. The fourth zone, the Negev Desert, lies in the south and covers nearly half of Israel.

The coastal plain is about 115 miles (185 km) long and 25 miles (40 km) wide.[6] It includes the beaches along the Mediterranean Sea and stretches of farmland to their east. Especially fertile is the Plain of Esdraelon, which is located in the north and is watered by the Qishon River. The coastal plain is the most densely populated area of Israel. Approximately half of all Israelis live there. The zone includes several important urban centers, including Tel Aviv and Haifa.

The surface of the Dead Sea is 1,414 feet (431 m) below sea level.[7]

MAP OF ISRAEL

LEBANON
SYRIA
N
W
E
S
Mount Meron
Haifa
Sea of Galilee
MEDITERRANEAN SEA
Jordan River
WEST BANK
Tel Aviv–Yafo
Yarqon River
Jerusalem
GAZA STRIP
Dead Sea
Beersheba
Malham Cave
EGYPT
JORDAN
Elat

KEY:

- Capital
- City
- Point of Interest

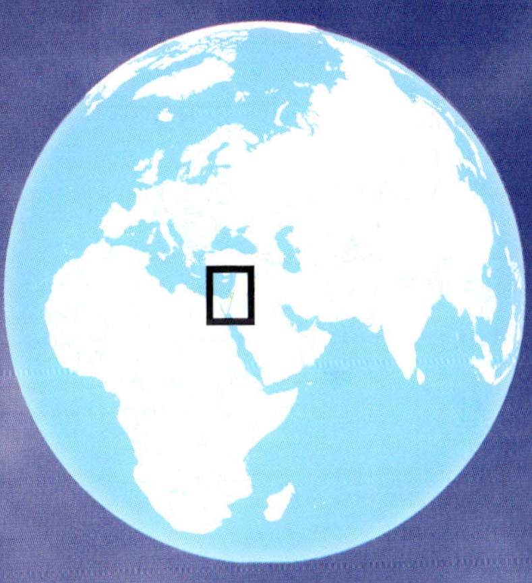

Mount Meron holds special significance in Judaism.

A DESERT RESORT

The Negev is too hot and dry to sustain a large population. Yet at its southern tip is the city of Elat, which is one of Israel's most active tourist destinations. The city is located on the Gulf of Elat, also called the Gulf of Aqaba, an arm of the Red Sea. Tourists flock to the city to swim, snorkel, and scuba dive in the gulf's warm waters.

The highlands of Galilee are found in north-central Israel. A series of mountain ranges run from the northern area of Galilee down to the Negev Desert. The hills and mountains of Galilee range from about 1,600 feet (488 m) to nearly 4,000 feet (1,219 m) above sea level.[8] The highest is Mount Meron, which stands at 3,963 feet (1,208 m).[9] The highlands zone includes the largely Arab city of Nazareth and the holy city of Jerusalem.

The Rift Valley zone is a narrow strip of land along Israel's eastern border. It is a part of the Great Rift Valley that stretches from Syria to Mozambique. The sides of the valley are steep, but its floor is relatively flat. Much of its floor is below sea level. The zone includes the Dead Sea, whose shores are the lowest point of land on Earth.

The Negev zone is a large arrowhead-shaped region in southern Israel. It makes up about half of the country's land area, but the landscape and climate are so forbidding that it is home to few people. The Negev includes flat, sandy desert lands, high mountains, and steep cliffs. In the south, the terrain features several crater-like landforms created by erosion, with the largest crater measuring five miles (8 km) across and 21 miles (34 km) long.[10]

RIVERS AND LAKES

Israel's rivers include the Yarqon and the Qishon, which empty into the Mediterranean Sea at Tel Aviv and Haifa, respectively. But the country's longest river is the Jordan, which flows north to south through the Rift Valley and ultimately into the Red Sea. The river is fairly narrow and shallow, though its waters rise during the rainy season.

The Jordan flows through Israel's largest lake, the Sea of Galilee. This body of water is also known as Lake Kinneret or Lake Tiberias. Measuring 5 miles (8 km) wide and 13 miles (21 km) long, the lake is a significant source of fresh water.[11] Another important Israeli lake is the Dead Sea. It is one of saltiest bodies of water in the world. Its waters are about ten times saltier than the ocean.

CLIMATE AND PRECIPITATION

In much of the country, Israelis enjoy a pleasant, moderate climate. The country has two main seasons—a dry, hot summer from June to October and a rainy, mild winter from November to May. Temperatures vary according to location and elevation. The hills and mountains of northern Galilee generally have the coldest temperatures. Sometimes in the winter, this region sees snowfall.

MALHAM CAVE

In southern Israel near the Dead Sea stands Mount Sodom. This 722-foot (220 m) hill is made of layers of salt covered with rock.[12] Inside Mount Sodom is Malham Cave, which researchers in 2019 determined is more than six miles (10 km) long, making it the longest salt cave in the world.[13] Its most stunning feature is the thousands of gleaming stalactites.

The area around the Dead Sea experiences sweltering temperatures in the summer.

On the other extreme is the Negev, where temperatures are higher than in the rest of the country. The coastal plain has the most comfortable weather conditions. Even in the hot summer, sea breezes cool the air, making the Mediterranean coast a favorite spot for vacationers.

Generally, January is Israel's coldest month, with high temperatures in Jerusalem averaging approximately 55 degrees Fahrenheit (13°C). The hottest month is usually August, with the temperature rising as high as 120 degrees Fahrenheit (49°C) at the Dead Sea.[14] In spring and fall, dry winds called khamsin sometimes blow in from the deserts to the east, causing the temperature to suddenly rise.

Israel sees most of its rainfall in the winter. The wettest areas are to the north. Upper Galilee receives about 44 inches (112 cm) of rain a year. The coastal plain sees less than half as much, averaging about 20 inches (51 cm) annually. It rarely rains at all in the Negev, especially in the south. There, annual rainfall is only about one inch (2.5 cm).[15]

THE WATER CRISIS

Israel faces several environmental challenges, including a lack of farmland, industrial pollution in the groundwater, and air pollution emitted from automobiles and factories. But its most pressing environmental crisis is a lack of fresh water due to low rainfall in much of the country. Families and businesses often face severe water shortages during the dry summer months.

Since its founding, the Israeli government has been working to solve its water problem. Training and recruiting many of the best water engineers, it has become a world leader in water management. One important initiative was developing technology to clean sewage water for reuse. Now about 90 percent of water in Israel's sewage system is recycled so it can be safely used

THE SHRINKING DEAD SEA

In recent decades, the water in the Dead Sea has been slowly disappearing. Its water level is dropping by about 40 inches (102 cm) each year.[16] The shrinking Dead Sea is a humanmade crisis. The sea is naturally replenished by water from the Jordan River, which is fed by the Sea of Galilee. But Israel and neighboring countries are diverting this water for use in homes, industries, and farms.

The Ashkelon Desalination Plant produces more than four billion cubic feet (118 million cubic m) of clean water in a year. Desalination is the process of removing salt from seawater so it's safe to drink.

to irrigate farms.[17] Israel has also had success with desalination efforts. By filtering out salt and other minerals, water engineers can turn seawater into usable fresh water.

The Israeli public also pitches in with water conservation efforts. Israelis welcome technologies that help them conserve water in their homes, in part because of the high cost of water to them personally. But they have also embraced water conservation as a virtue, a cultural value promoted by the government's water policies. As early as kindergarten, schoolchildren are taught about water efficiency and about how to play their part in solving Israel's water crisis.

CHAPTER **THREE**

PLANTS AND ANIMALS

The Old Testament of the Bible, known to Jews as the Hebrew Bible, describes ancient Israel as "a land of wheat and barley and vines and fig-trees and pomegranates, a land of olive oil and honey."[1] The modern nation of Israel remains a land of plenty. With its varied terrain and mix of habitats, the country can sustain many types of living things.

VARIED VEGETATION

Forests cover about 7 percent of Israel.[2] The land's original evergreen forests were decimated by centuries of overcutting and clearing land for agriculture. The government, however, has made restoring forests a

Israel has relatively few forested areas, but these regions contain diverse plant and animal life.

The anemone, Israel's national flower, can be identified by its bright-red petals.

priority and is responsible for the planting of millions of new trees, especially oak trees and small evergreens. In the Galilean highlands, almond and olive trees are cultivated, while the coastal plain is fertile ground for orange trees and other citrus fruit trees. In the Jordan River valley, trees produce bananas, avocados, and mangoes. Even in the sunbaked Negev, date palms can thrive if they have a source of underground water.

During the rainy season, the highlands are filled with color as wildflowers begin to bloom. Flowers such as rockroses, crocuses, and hyacinths blanket entire hillsides. A favorite wildflower in Israel is the anemone, which has been designated the national flower. In the early spring, red anemones carpet the plains of the northern Negev. An annual festival called Darom Adom (meaning "red south") invites visitors to experience the anemones in all their glory. The festival also features nature walks, picnicking, and hot-air balloon rides.

Some of the most popular cultivated flowers in the world originated in lands along the Mediterranean Sea. They include the cyclamen, which thrives in Israel's woodlands and hillsides. The narcissus is another favorite that grows wild in several regions of Israel, including the northern mountains and coastal plains. The rugged narcissus can also be found in rock pockets in the highlands of the Negev.

SAVING THE WILDFLOWERS

Israelis used to pick wildflowers, either to decorate their homes or to sell to others. In 1963, Israel outlawed the practice because many flowering species were facing extinction. A public relations campaign posted some 30,000 colorful posters in schools and other public locations, urging people not to pick or sell flowers.[4] The highly successful campaign helped save Israel's wildflowers for generations to come.

MAMMALS, LARGE AND SMALL

Israel is home to 116 species of mammals.[3] Among the largest are wild boars, leopards, wolves, jackals,

The Nubian ibex is known for its large, curved horns.

foxes, and hyenas. Mountain gazelles thrive in dry, desert areas. These spindly-legged animals have a brown coat and distinctive white markings near their eyes. Rare for mammals, both males and females have horns. Caracals are large felines with high tufted ears. Most active at night, caracals live on the ground but are skilled at climbing trees. Another notable large mammal of Israel is the Nubian ibex, which is well-adapted to hot climates. The male ibex sports a dark-brown beard and enormous horns that grow in a circular shape.

Smaller mammals in Israel include hares, badgers, hedgehogs, voles, mice, martens, and porcupines. Indian porcupines found in Israel are larger than their North American counterparts. Their quills can grow to 16 inches (41 cm) long, and their strong front paws are powerful tools for digging underground burrows.[5] Honey badgers are largely solitary creatures that tend to act aggressively when confronted. They have black fur marked by a gray or white stripe down the back and tail. Sand cats have light tan fur that helps them hide in their desert environment. Their large, furry paws allow them to walk comfortably on hot sand.

SKY AND SEA

More than 400 species of birds live in Israel.[6] They include sand grouses, partridges, bustards, desert larks, and tropical cuckoos. Among the birds of prey native to the country are falcons, hawks, kestrels, spotted eagles, and long-legged buzzards.

Two times a year, Israel's bird population skyrockets as many species make their annual migrations. In the fall, birds from Europe and Asia migrate south to spend the winter in Africa, and in the spring, they return north to their breeding grounds. Both ways, many stop at the Hula Valley in northern Israel, making the area ideal for bird-watching. The migration paths are so predictable that airplanes are forbidden from flying there when the birds are expected.

The lakes, rivers, and coastal waters of Israel are home to many fish species and other aquatic creatures. The widest variety can be found at the coral reef near the coastal city of Elat. In addition to corals, sponges, and shellfish, there are thousands of species of fish and mollusks living there. Frequent visitors to the reef include whale sharks, dolphins, and migrating birds. The adjoining beach is also a nesting site for hawksbill sea turtles.

THE CANAAN DOG

Distinguished by its erect ears and bushy curled tail, the Canaan dog is the national dog of Israel. Archaeological evidence suggests that the Canaan dog has lived in what is now Israel for more than 1,000 years. Able to thrive in high temperatures with little water, the animal is well suited to desert environments. Today, the Israeli military trains these highly intelligent dogs to sniff out land mines.

Because of restoration efforts, the Hula Nature Reserve was designated as a Wetland of International Importance in 1996.

PRESERVING NATURAL HABITATS

Israel has almost 100 species of reptiles, including geckos, lizards, and vipers.[7] But there are only seven known species of amphibians in the country.[8] They live mainly along the Mediterranean coast, where they can breed in small ponds. The wetlands of the Hula Valley in Galilee had once been an even more hospitable environment for amphibians. But in the 1950s, the government drained the swamps there to create farmland. However, this destroyed the natural habitat of many animal species. Recognizing the environmental damage the project had created, the government began efforts to restore part of the wetlands in the 1990s.

Every year, as many as 500 million migrating birds visit Israel.[9]

A wide variety of raptors, such as the griffon vulture, nest in the Gamla Nature Reserve in northern Israel.

Another longstanding threat to wildlife in Israel is a culture of hunting. Since the 1800s, hunters have been responsible for killing off several notable species, including the Arabian oryx, Syrian bear, and Nile crocodile. Modern Israel has sharply restricted hunting, requiring hunters to file for permits and prohibiting the killing of certain animals.

Israel's rapidly growing population and increased industrial development also pose a threat to the nation's wildlife. To protect natural habitats, the government has designated about one-fourth of Israel's land area as nature reserves and national parks. These protected areas allow visitors to see some of the country's most spectacular flora and fauna. For instance, the En Gedi Nature Reserve is populated with ibex, hyraxes, wolves, hyenas, and spotted leopards, while the Gamla Nature Reserve, the site of Israel's highest waterfall, is the home of dozens of pairs of griffon vultures. Two nature reserves are devoted to restoring native species. The Hai-Bar Yotvata Nature Reserve and the Hai-Bar Carmel Nature Reserve are raising Asian wild asses, Arabian oryx, and Persian fallow deer, among other species, with the hope of one day releasing them into the wild.

BUNKERS FOR BATS

After a 1994 peace agreement, the Israeli army abandoned underground bunkers it had built along the Jordan River. People were forbidden from entering the area. But that did not stop more than a dozen bat species from moving in to the bunkers. Several species had been at risk of becoming extinct before finding this unusual habitat. One researcher noted, "There is no doubt that by being in a closed military zone that has prevented human interference, the bat habitat will allow these delicate creatures to thrive."[10]

CHAPTER **FOUR**

HISTORY

In what is now Israel, archaeologists have found some of the oldest fossils indicating human habitation. It is possible that human beings first lived in the area 185,000 years ago. Agriculture was introduced by about 4000 BCE, and trading towns grew up by approximately 3000 BCE. About 1,200 years later, Hebrew people, who became known as Israelites, began arriving in the area.

BATTLING INVADERS

According to biblical tradition, a group of Israelites led by Moses escaped servitude in Egypt by fleeing to what is now Israel, a land promised to them by God. In about 1000 BCE, the Israelites were united by King David, who ruled from the city of Jerusalem. His son Solomon built

Israeli archaeologists displayed several important finds in 2021. This included a large basket found near the Dead Sea that is estimated to be 10,500 years old.

In art, King David is often depicted playing a harp.

the First Temple there. After his reign ended, the kingdom was split into Israel in the north and Judah in the south. From *Judah* came the word *Jew,* the name the Israelites became known as.

Historical writings and archaeological evidence recount that the Israelites' homeland was repeatedly invaded by great powers. The Assyrians took over Israel, and the Babylonians conquered Judah and destroyed the temple. Many Jews were exiled, although some were able to return to Jerusalem after the Persians conquered Babylonia. This exile marked the beginning of the Jewish Diaspora, when the Jewish people dispersed to lands around the world to live among non-Jews.

In 167 BCE, the Jews rebelled against the Seleucids, who then controlled the region, and revived the kingdom of Judah. About 100 years later, the Romans invaded Judah. In 70 CE they destroyed the Second Temple, and in 135 they drove the Jews from Jerusalem. The region, which was now called Palestine after a Roman word for the area, fell to Muslim Arabs in the 600s. Christian crusaders conquered Jerusalem in 1099 but lost the city to Muslim ruler Saladin in 1187. The Ottoman Empire took control of Palestine in 1516 and ruled the area until the beginning of the 1900s. During this time, Palestine's population was made up largely of Muslim and Christian Arabs, although there were small Jewish communities in Jerusalem and other urban areas.

THE ZIONIST MOVEMENT

By the 1800s, only about 25,000 Jews lived in Palestine.[1] The Zionist movement, led by Austrian journalist Theodor Herzl, sought to greatly increase that number. Herzl and other Zionists were alarmed by growing European anti-Semitism. They wanted to create a new state in Palestine for the Jewish people, where they would be safe from the discrimination, prejudice, and violence they were experiencing in the countries where they lived. Prominent Zionist Chaim Weizmann encouraged Jews to immigrate to Palestine in support of Zionism. As more and more Jews began moving there, tensions flared between the Jewish immigrants and Palestinian Arabs who had long called the area home.

During World War I (1914–1918), the Ottoman Empire collapsed, and the United Kingdom gained control over Palestine. Zionists persuaded the British to issue the Balfour Declaration, which promoted the idea of a Jewish homeland in the region. Arab Palestinians were outraged, leading to the Arab Revolt of 1936–1939. During this uprising, Arab rebels attacked Jewish settlements and

Theodor Herzl was among the most prominent voices pushing for the establishment of a Jewish state in Palestine.

British outposts. The British were surprised by the Arab determination to retake control of Palestine. This conflict also saw the rise of several Jewish militia groups, which included future Israeli political leaders such as prime ministers Yitzhak Rabin, Menachem Begin, and Yitzhak Shamir.

European immigration to Palestine soared in the 1930s as Jews tried to escape the brutal anti-Semitic persecution of Germany's Nazi regime. The British restricted Jewish immigration in an effort to retain Arab support during World War II (1939–1945). Nevertheless, by the end of the war in 1945, about 600,000 Jews were living in Palestine.[2] In the aftermath of the devastating war, the world was shocked by the extent of Nazi Germany's systematic murder of the Jewish people. Horror over this act of genocide, which is known as the Holocaust, increased the pressure on the United Kingdom to create a Jewish state in Palestine.

ISRAEL BECOMES A NATION

In 1947, Arab and Jewish leaders met at a peace conference in London, but they could not reach an agreement. The British then turned the problem of Palestine over to the United Nations (UN), the international peacekeeping organization founded after World War II to prevent future conflicts. The UN voted to divide Palestine into two states. One would be Jewish, and the other would be Arab. The city of Jerusalem would become an international zone. Zionist leaders approved the plan, but Arab leaders rejected it, maintaining that the proposed Arab state would not provide enough territory for their people.

On May 14, 1948, the day before the British Mandate establishing British rule over Palestine was set to expire, Jewish leaders proclaimed that Israel was an independent nation. It became the first Jewish state to exist in 2,000 years. To support the Palestinian Arabs, armies from five Arab nations—Egypt, Syria, Iraq, Lebanon, and Transjordan (now Jordan)—immediately invaded. During the conflict, the Arab forces had many more soldiers, but they were not trained or organized well. Although outnumbered, the Israeli troops managed to repel repeated Arab attacks.

Out of a population of approximately 1.2 million Palestinian Arabs living in Israel before the nation's independence, some 750,000 were forced to flee their homes after the conflict.[4]

Between February and July 1949, Israel negotiated separate peace agreements with the five Arab nations. At the end of the war, Israel held one-fifth more territory than it would have controlled under the UN proposal.[3] Israel's lands

Political leaders of the new state of Israel commemorated the nation's founding at the Tel Aviv Art Museum on May 14, 1948.

included West Jerusalem. Jordan annexed East Jerusalem and a region along the Jordan River designated as the West Bank. Egypt took control of an area known as the Gaza Strip. Many Palestinians in Israel were forced to relocate to refugee camps in Gaza, the West Bank, Lebanon, and Syria. The victorious Israelis called the conflict the War for Independence. The Arabs called it the Nakba, meaning "catastrophe."

A YOUNG COUNTRY

By winning the war, Israel had survived its first great threat as a nation. But immediately it faced many more challenges. Neighboring Arab states refused to formally recognize Israel and implemented an economic boycott against the new nation. In its early years, Israel struggled economically, relying largely on assistance from Jewish charities and aid from the US government, which gave the powerful United States influence over Israel's political landscape.

Even though the war was over, the potential for violence remained. Israel felt the constant threat of a possible attack or invasion by these adversaries. Also unresolved were the conflicts between Jewish Israelis and the remaining Palestinian Arab

THE LAW OF RETURN

To increase its population, the Israeli government passed the Law of Return in 1950. This law declared, "Every Jew has the right to come to this country as an *oleh*." *Oleh* means "Jewish immigrant." A later amendment defined a Jew as "a person who was born of a Jewish mother or has become converted to Judaism and who is not a member of another religion" and established immigration rights for spouses, children, and grandchildren of Jews.[5]

population. Israelis' relations with the residents of the Arab settlements in the West Bank and Gaza were especially volatile.

To retain its land claims, Israel encouraged Jewish people the world over to immigrate there. Approximately 250,000 of the immigrants who responded were survivors of the Holocaust.[6] Many others were Jews from countries in the Middle East and northern Africa. They were classified as Mizrahim (also called Sephardic Jews), as opposed to Ashkenazim, Jews who had emigrated from European countries. Friction between the more well-established Ashkenazim and the newly arrived Mizrahim caused significant strain within Israel's evolving society.

WAR AND PEACE

From the late 1950s to the early 1970s, Israel was involved in three major conflicts with Egypt and other Arab states. With the backing of the United Kingdom and France, Israel invaded Egypt in 1956 in retaliation for Egypt nationalizing the Suez Canal. Israel withdrew its troops the following year. In 1967 came a conflict known as the Six-Day War. Israel again attacked Egypt. Jordan and Syria quickly joined the conflict. After Israel destroyed Egypt's air

THE MUNICH OLYMPICS MASSACRE

The greatest tragedy ever to occur at the Olympic Games happened in Munich, Germany, in 1972. Eight Palestinian militants with the group Black September invaded the Olympic Village. They found the apartments of the Israeli Olympic team, where they shot and killed a coach and one athlete and took nine others hostage. Local police staged a rescue attempt, but in the midst of its botched execution, all of the hostages were killed, along with five of the terrorists.

Israeli troops moved into battle in the Sinai Peninsula during the Six-Day War.

force, its ground forces managed to gain control of a substantial amount of new territory. By the end of the war, Israel had taken the Golan Heights from Syria, the Gaza Strip and Sinai Peninsula from Egypt, and the West Bank from Jordan. Israel's victory also secured its control over all of Jerusalem.

Egypt and Syria launched a surprise attack on Israel in 1973 on Yom Kippur, the Jewish holy day of atonement. The Israel Defense Forces (IDF) suffered heavy casualties in the initial fighting. However, they quickly regrouped, and a ceasefire agreement ended the war after just a few weeks.

The hostilities between Israel and Egypt came to an end in 1978 with the Camp David Accords. Under pressure from the United States, Israeli prime minister Menachem Begin met with Egyptian president Anwar Sadat at the American presidential retreat known as Camp David. Their negotiations resulted in a peace treaty in which Israel agreed to return the Sinai Peninsula to Egypt. It also established diplomatic relations between the two countries. For their role in the Camp David Accords, Begin and Sadat were awarded the 1978 Nobel Peace Prize.

THE OSLO ACCORDS

Under the peace agreement, Israel withdrew from the Sinai Peninsula in 1982. Just weeks later, though, the country was mired in another conflict. This time it was with the Palestine Liberation Organization (PLO), a political organization that represented Palestinians opposed to the state of Israel. The PLO had been engaging in guerrilla attacks on Israel for decades.

In order to expel PLO leadership from its strongholds in Lebanon, the IDF bombed and invaded the country. During the conflict, the Israeli military allowed a militia to massacre Palestinians in two refugee camps. The scandal surrounding the massacre sent Israelis into the streets during mass protests against their government and forced Prime Minister Begin to resign. The IDF eventually withdrew from Lebanon in June 1985.

Violence broke out between Israelis and Palestinians during the first intifada.

Meanwhile, frustration among the Palestinians in the territories occupied by the Israeli military was growing to a fever pitch. It exploded into widespread protest and violence in late 1987, the beginning of what became known as the first intifada. *Intifada* is an Arabic word meaning "shaking off." Palestinians, many in their teens, began confronting and throwing rocks at Israeli soldiers, who fought back. Media images of Israeli soldiers attacking Palestinian civilians amid the escalating violence drew criticism from around the world.

In the 1990s, international pressure mounted for a resolution of the Israeli-Palestinian conflict, especially after Yasser Arafat, the leader of the PLO, said that his organization would be willing to end the violence and recognize Israel as a legitimate country in exchange for a Palestinian state. The administration of Prime Minister Yitzhak Rabin began secret negotiations with PLO leaders in Oslo, Norway. The result was a series of agreements known as the Oslo Accords. They outlined a five-year plan to end Israeli military presence in the occupied Palestinian territories and to gradually implement Palestinian self-rule, possibly leading to the formation of a Palestinian state. In exchange, the PLO pledged to end terrorism directed against Israelis. In 1994, Israel began withdrawing from much of Gaza and the city of Jericho in the West Bank, while the PLO formed the Palestinian National Authority as a governing body for formerly occupied Palestinian areas. That year also saw the signing of a historic peace treaty between Israel and its former adversary Jordan.

Many Israelis supported the peace negotiations. But militant Palestinians opposed the Oslo Accords,

THE PALESTINIAN NATIONAL AUTHORITY

Following the Oslo Accords of the 1990s, the Palestinian Authority (later renamed the Palestinian National Authority) was formed. It was meant to be a temporary Palestinian government charged with managing the Palestinian territories in the West Bank and Gaza until Palestine and Israel solidified a peace deal. Peace negotiations stalled, leaving the Palestinian National Authority in place. It is controlled by the political party Fatah. The party is a rival of the militant group Hamas, which now controls Gaza. The fraught relationship between Fatah and Hamas presents yet another challenge to negotiating a lasting peace.

as did Israeli hardliners, who did not want to make any concessions to the Palestinians. The agreements were also denounced by Jewish settlers in the occupied territories. For decades, the government had supported the establishment of Jewish settlements in the West Bank and other disputed areas in an effort to isolate Arab towns and make the creation of a Palestinian state more difficult. Outrage over the Oslo Accords drove an extremist right-wing Jewish student to assassinate Prime Minister Rabin in 1995.

As the years passed, negotiations between the Israelis and Palestinians bogged down over a series of difficult issues, including the status of Jerusalem, the borders of the Palestinian state, the future of Jewish settlers in the West Bank, and the fate of Palestinian refugees. The lack of progress led to the second intifada from 2000 to 2005. Violence also repeatedly broke out along the border of Gaza in the latter half of the decade after the militant Islamic organization Hamas took over the region. Israel became embroiled in still another conflict in 2006, when the IDF battled the militant group Hezbollah in the Second Lebanon War.

THE NETANYAHU ERA

As Israel headed into the 2000s, its most influential leader was Benjamin Netanyahu. A member of the conservative Likud Party, he served as prime minister from 1996 to 1999 and again from 2009 to 2021, making him Israel's longest-serving leader. Netanyahu oversaw a booming economy. At the same time, his critics charged that he exploited deep divisions in Israeli society and failed to prioritize the peace process with the Palestinians.

Netanyahu, *left*, maintained a friendly relationship with US president Donald Trump, visiting the United States several times during the Trump administration.

Late in US president Barack Obama's second term, the United States passed its largest military aid package to Israel in history, allocating about $38 billion over ten years.[7] Yet Netanyahu was less deferential to the US president than past prime ministers had been. For instance, he publicly denounced President Obama's nuclear deal with Iran, designed to slow Iran's nuclear weapons program in exchange for lifting sanctions on the country. Netanyahu had a more cordial relationship with fellow conservative President Donald Trump. In December 2017, President Trump went against US precedent and the international community by recognizing Jerusalem as Israel's capital, supporting Israel's claims on the city. In November 2019, Trump also announced that the United States no longer regarded Jewish settlements in the West Bank to be illegal.

With American support, Netanyahu's government signed agreements normalizing relations with Bahrain, Morocco, and the United Arab Emirates in 2020. It also cultivated ties with other countries in Asia, Africa, and Latin America. These new alliances meant that Israel was becoming less dependent on the United States and its traditional allies in Europe. Some analysts noted that this made Israel more immune to demands for a peaceful resolution of the Israeli-Palestinian conflict. With violence at a relatively low level in the West Bank, Netanyahu was able to marginalize the issue and refused to make any significant concessions. Polling in 2020 showed that growing numbers of Jewish Israelis were also largely indifferent to the peace process. In 2019, Netanyahu was charged with bribery, fraud, and breach of trust. Despite the charges, he continued serving as prime minister until June 2021, when a new governing coalition led by Naftali Bennett ousted him from power.

CHAPTER **FIVE**

PEOPLE AND CULTURE

Israel has an incredibly diverse population. Its policy of inviting Jews from across the world to immigrate there has created a society of people from a wide array of cultures and backgrounds. In many ways, Israel has had enormous success absorbing people with differing beliefs and values. However, while the ethnic, religious, and cultural divisions help to create a vibrant society, they also are sometimes a source of tension and conflict.

JEWISH ISRAELIS

Jewish people make up about three-quarters of Israel's population of nearly nine million.[1] They trace their

Israel has a unique mix of religions, languages, cuisines, and cultures.

ancestries from all corners of the globe, including Europe, North America, the Middle East, North Africa, central Asia, and Latin America.

Most Jewish immigrants to Israel have been traditionally classified into two large groups: Ashkenazi Jews and Mizrahi Jews. Ashkenazim come from central and eastern European, while Mizrahim have roots in other Middle Eastern countries and northern Africa. The Israelis who founded the country were primarily Ashkenazim. As a result, they have tended to hold top positions in Israeli society and politics. The Mizrahim, who largely arrived in the 1950s and later, were generally less affluent and educated when they immigrated. They sometimes felt the Ashkenazim looked down on them and came to resent the Ashkenazim's privileges. In recent years, though, the traditional tensions between these groups have eased as the Mizrahim have made professional and educational advances.

Another distinct group of Israeli Jews are the Beta Israel, or Ethiopian Jews. In the 1980s and 1990s, the Israeli government arranged for about 90,000 Jews to emigrate from Ethiopia in order to escape civil war and famine.[2] Although initially welcomed, Ethiopian Jews have struggled to thrive in Israel, where they have often faced racism and discrimination. They remain the most impoverished segment of the Jewish population.

Another recent wave of immigration brought approximately one million Jews from the former Soviet Union to Israel beginning in the 1990s. This mass influx of people transformed many cities and played a role in realigning the Israeli political scene, as Russian immigrants tended to support right-wing policies, particularly regarding the Israeli-Palestinian conflict. Russian Jews often prefer

Religious practices, including prayer gatherings, are an important part of daily life for many Israeli Jews.

socializing with one another, allowing them to retain many cultural elements from life in their old country.

Within Israel, there are also several small, distinct Jewish communities. For instance, a few thousand Israeli Jews are Karaites. They belong to a sect of Judaism that dates from the Middle Ages. Although they are considered part of Jewish society, they live in isolated communities and

generally do not marry outside their group. The Karaites live primarily in the cities of Beersheba, Ramla, and Ashdod.

Another small Jewish minority are the Samaritans. They trace their roots to the Jewish population that remained in what is now Israel after the Assyrians conquered the region in the 700s BCE. Several hundred Samaritans live in the town of Holon near Tel Aviv and on Mount Gerizim in the West Bank. While praying they speak an ancient dialect of Hebrew, but otherwise they communicate in Arabic.

SABRAS

Today, more than 70 percent of Jewish Israelis were born in Israel.[3] They are proud to be known by the nickname "Sabras." It is derived from the similar Arabic and Hebrew words for a prickly pear cactus, whose thick skin covers its soft, sweet flesh. The name is a joke on how Israeli-born Jews see themselves—tough and blustery on the outside, but sweet and kind at heart.

OBSERVING THE FAITH

All practicing Jews in Israel share some common religious beliefs. They worship a single god to whom the Jews are the chosen people. Their sacred text is the Hebrew Bible, with special importance placed on its first five books, known to Jews as the Torah. They come together to worship at synagogues and observe the weekly Sabbath from sunset on Friday to nightfall on Saturday. They also participate in Jewish holidays, such as Yom Kippur, Rosh Hashana, and Passover.

How Israeli Jews engage with Judaism ranges from extremely observant to nonobservant. About half regard themselves as secular, or nonreligious. While the practice of Judaism does not play an important role in their daily lives, secular Jews may occasionally go to synagogue, observe religious holidays, and attend a family dinner on the Sabbath. Most practicing Jews fall into three denominations. These, listed from the least to the most observant of religious tenets and laws, are Reform, Conservative, and Orthodox.

Jews living in Israel make up about 45 percent of the world's total Jewish population.[5]

About 8 percent of Israeli Jews are called ultra-Orthodox.[4] Known as the Haredi, their entire lives revolve around Judaism. They strictly follow religious laws and devote much of their time to religious study. The Haredi usually live in their own segregated neighborhoods, wear traditional clothing, and separate men and women in public life.

ARABS IN ISRAEL

Palestinian Arabs make up most of Israel's non-Jewish population. They live primarily in the north and in Arab neighborhoods in cities and towns such as Jerusalem, Haifa, and Ramla. Arabs are the largest share of the population in some towns, most notably Nazareth in Galilee. The population of the occupied West Bank is also largely Arab.

Some Bedouin people live in villages rather than living in the traditional nomadic lifestyle.

The Negev is the home of the Bedouin, who make up roughly one-tenth of Israel's Arab population. Traditionally, the Bedouin were a nomadic people who raised herds of sheep and goats in the desert. For years, the Israeli government has tried to move the Bedouin to permanent settlements, leading to frequent confrontations between officials and the Bedouin.

Most Arabs in Israel are Muslims, adherents to the Islamic faith. Islam was founded in the 600s CE by the prophet Muhammad. Muslims believe in a single god, known as Allah. They believe that the Quran, the holy book of Islam, contains the words of Allah as communicated to Muhammad. Devout Muslims pray in the direction of the holy city of Mecca five times a day and gather at mosques, Islamic houses of worship, to pray on Fridays. The majority of Israeli Arabs are Sunni Muslims, members of one of the two major branches of Islam.

THE CIRCASSIANS

About 4,000 non-Arab Sunni Muslims in Israel are members of the Circassian ethnic group.[8] Their ancestors were war refugees who fled the Caucasus Mountains in the late 1800s. The Circassians are concentrated in two mostly Circassian villages, Kfar Kama and Rehaniya, both in Galilee. The Circassians are the only Muslim community where men are compelled to serve in Israel's military.

CHRISTIANS AND OTHER RELIGIOUS MINORITIES

Christians make up about 2 percent of the Israeli population.[6] The majority are Arabs. The largest denominations are the Greek Catholic church and the Greek Orthodox church. Smaller denominations include Evangelicals, Episcopalians, and Lutherans.

People belonging to the Druze religious sect make up about 1.6 percent of the Israeli population.[7] With roots in Islam, this religion was established in Egypt in the 1010s CE. Recognized as Arabs by the Israeli government, the Druze are mostly found in villages in Galilee and near Mount Carmel in Haifa.

Other members of a religious minority in Israel include several hundred residents who adhere to the Baha'i faith. This religion was founded in the mid-1800s in Iran. The worldwide headquarters and central shrine of this faith are located on Israel's Mount Carmel.

Street signs in Israel often include Hebrew, Arabic, and English.

HEBREW AND ARABIC

The official language of Israel is Modern Hebrew. This form of Hebrew is a relatively new language. It was invented by Eliezer Ben-Yehuda, a lexicographer who moved to Jerusalem in the 1880s. He pledged that his family in its new home would speak only Hebrew. Since the Jewish Diaspora 2,000 years earlier, Hebrew had been used only in religious rituals and writings. Because of the limited vocabulary of ancient Hebrew, Yehuda began to coin new words needed for the modern world. He eventually compiled a dictionary, which became the basis of the language most Israelis now speak.

Although Arabic is not an official language of Israel, it holds special status under Israeli law. Arabic is mostly spoken by the Arab minority. Some Arabs, especially young people, also speak Hebrew because it helps them in larger society. Many Israelis also know English, which is taught in schools and commonly used in business dealings. Immigrants in Israel sometimes use the languages of their homelands with family and friends. Because of the large number of immigrants from the former Soviet Union, it is not unusual to hear Russian spoken in Israel.

THE CULTURAL SCENE

The arts in Israel are as diverse as its people. Its music, literature, and theater reflect aspects of the many home cultures of its immigrant population. At the same time, artists make an effort to develop uniquely Israeli works, often by using their art to comment on Jewish history and on modern Israeli life.

In urban centers, the many art galleries, concert halls, theaters, libraries, and museums are a testament to Israel's thriving cultural scene. Notable cultural institutions include the Israel Museum, which is a center for biblical and historical research, and the Academy of the Hebrew Language, which studies the use of the national language. Israel's oldest art museum, the Tel Aviv Museum of Art, showcases modern and contemporary works by both Israeli and foreign artists.

Perhaps Israel's most treasured cultural institution is the Israel Philharmonic Orchestra, which holds its performances at the Mann Auditorium in Tel Aviv. Classical music was introduced to the area in the 1930s by musicians immigrating from Europe. Listening to classical music has become a very popular pastime. The international renown of homegrown musicians including pianist Daniel Barenboim and violinists Itzhak Perlman and Pinchas Zukerman is a source of pride for Israeli music lovers.

THE ARTS

Painting and sculpture in Israel are largely influenced by the work of European artists. Since the 1950s, the artists of the New Horizon group have been well-known for their abstract landscapes. Paintings with biblical themes and local images are also popular. Israeli craftspeople handmake a variety of objects, including menorahs, spice boxes, and mezuzahs, parchment scrolls with religious texts that are commonly attached to doorposts outside Jewish homes.

Israel is home to many ballet and modern dance troupes, but folk dancing is the type of dance most associated with the country. Ashkenazi Jews, Mizrahi Jews, and Palestinian Arabs all have rich folk dancing traditions. Aside from classical music, Israelis enjoy a variety of contemporary music genres, including pop, techno, and hip-hop. Listening to concerts at outdoor venues such as HaYarkon Park and Caesarea Amphitheater is a favorite summertime activity.

Attending professional and amateur theatrical productions is also popular in Israel. The national theater of Israel since 1958, the Habima stages classical and contemporary plays by Israeli and foreign playwrights. Israeli film and television offer dramas and comedies about modern Israel and its people. Modern standouts in the Israeli entertainment industry are actress Gal Gadot, famous for playing Wonder Woman, and director Nadav Lapid, whose 2019 film *Synonyms* was awarded the Golden Bear for best film at the Berlin International Film Festival.

Despite the short history of the Modern Hebrew language, Hebrew literature is rich in its quality and scope. One of Israel's most celebrated writers is Shmuel Yosef Agnon, whose short stories and novels won him the Nobel Prize in Literature in 1966. Amos Oz received international

MINI **BIO**

GAL GADOT

After her breakout in the 2017 movie *Wonder Woman*, the *Times of Israel* speculated that actress Gal Gadot might become the "biggest Israeli superstar ever."[9] Born in 1985, she was raised in the small Israeli city of Rosh Ha'ayin. On a whim, at age 18 she began entering beauty pageants. To her surprise, she won the title of Miss Israel in 2004, and she went on to compete in the Miss Universe pageant. She worked as a model before serving in the IDF at age 20. For months, she studied Krav Maga, the IDF's famed self-defense training, before becoming a combat trainer. As she later recalled, "The soldiers loved me because I made them fit."[10]

After leaving the IDF, Gadot got into acting. She starred in the Israeli television drama *Bubot* before winning a role in the *Fast and Furious* movie franchise. Gadot says she got the part because her military training and knowledge of weapons impressed the director. Her physicality also helped her embody the superhero Wonder Woman, a role that made her a global movie star and one of Israel's favorite celebrities.

Gal Gadot has become one of the biggest action stars in the world.

Thousands of fans filled HaYarkon Park in 2011 to see pop star Justin Bieber, one of many major musical acts who have appeared at the outdoor venue.

acclaim for his ironic view of Israeli life in his novels, as well as in his memoir *A Tale of Love and Darkness*. Sayed Kashua is one of the best known Arab Israeli writers, both for his novels, including *Dancing Arabs* and *Track Changes*, and for the columns he wrote for the popular Israeli newspaper *Ha'aretz*.

EATING WELL

The cuisine of Israel is a delicious mix of regional dishes. Probably the most popular food is falafel, which consists of balls of ground chickpeas deep-fried to create a crunchy crust. Falafel is often topped with pickled vegetables and hummus, which is a chickpea spread, or tahini, a sesame seed sauce. Falafel vendors are everywhere, ready to serve a quick street meal. In Tel Aviv, a street called Shuk Betzalel is devoted to falafel vendors.

Other favorite foods include shawarma, roasted meat stuffed in a pita; *sabich*, a pita filled with fried eggplant, hard-boiled egg, and tahini; kebabs, which are meat and vegetables grilled and served on a skewer; and *burekas*, pastries filled with spinach, potato, or cheese. Israelis also enjoy vegetable salads dressed with olive oil and lemon juice, fruits and fruit juices, cheese, and yogurt. Some popular foreign

Falafel, which is often served in a pita, is one of the foods most closely linked with Israel.

foods include Russian borscht, which is a type of beet soup, and American favorites such as pizza and hamburgers.

Many Israelis observe religious dietary rules. Jews often follow kosher law, which prohibits them from eating certain animals, including pigs, hares, lobsters, oysters, shrimp, and clams, and from combining meat and dairy in the same meal. Muslims do not eat pork or drink alcohol. Dietary rules for both Jews and Muslims call for animals to be slaughtered in ritual manners that show the creatures compassion and respect.

CELEBRATING HOLIDAYS

Every year, Israelis celebrate Independence Day to commemorate Israel's founding as a nation on May 14, 1948. The date of this holiday, as with other holidays in the country, changes from year to year because Israel uses the Hebrew calendar. The Independence Day celebration is marked with military parades.

Other national holidays in Israel are Jewish religious commemorations. Among the most important Jewish holidays are Rosh Hashanah, which is the Jewish New Year, and Yom Kippur, the Day of Atonement. Yom Kippur is a solemn occasion, and religious Jews spend the day fasting. Sukkot, or the Feast of the Tabernacles, takes place over eight days. Families build shelters called sukkot in their yards to commemorate the lodgings of the early Israelites in the desert. Israeli Jews celebrate Pesach, or Passover, over seven days. On the first night, families recall the biblical Exodus of the Jews from Egypt and share a holiday meal called a seder.

Israeli Arabs celebrate the holiday of Eid al-Fitr at the end of Ramadan. Some relax during this time by visiting the beaches of Tel Aviv.

Muslims and Christians observe their own religious holidays as well. For Muslims, these include the month-long observation of Ramadan, during which Muslims fast in daylight hours. Ramadan ends with the joyful celebration of Eid al-Fitr. On another holiday, Eid al-Adha, Muslims commemorate the story from the Quran of Ibrahim's willingness to sacrifice his son for Allah. Christians in Israel celebrate Easter and Christmas. On Christmas Eve, a choir traditionally performs at Manger Square in Bethlehem, the city of Jesus's birth.

SPORTS AND GAMES

Many Israelis are sports lovers, either as amateur athletes or as fans of professional teams. The most popular sport is soccer, closely followed by basketball, which was introduced to Israel by American immigrants. The team Maccabi Playtika Tel Aviv is a basketball powerhouse that has won six championships playing European teams in the EuroLeague.[11]

Other sports enjoyed in Israel include volleyball, handball, boxing, tennis, wrestling, karate, and swimming. A favorite beach sport is *matkot*. In this type of paddleball, two players bat a small rubber ball back and forth, working together to keep the ball from falling on the sand.

Another physical activity created in Israel is Krav Maga. This form of self-defense training was invented by the IDF. Krav Maga combines moves from wrestling, boxing, and jujitsu. When used by soldiers, the goal of Krav Maga is to do anything to stay alive and subdue an adversary. For civilians at the gym, it provides an exhilarating workout while building self-defense skills.

THE MACCABIAH GAMES

Every four years, thousands of Jewish athletes from more than 80 countries meet in Israel to compete in the Maccabiah Games.[12] Nicknamed the Jewish Olympics, it is the third-largest sporting event in the world. The fields of competition include basketball, cricket, fencing, golf, ice hockey, karate, rugby, surfing, tennis, water polo, and weightlifting. The games also feature chess competitions.

An Israeli woman undergoes Krav Maga training at a gym. This martial art is designed for self-defense, and it is meant to be used only after all attempts to avoid conflict have failed.

CHAPTER **SIX**

POLITICS

The State of Israel has no formal constitution. Instead, the structure of its government is defined by the Basic Laws. According to this group of laws, Israel is a parliamentary democracy. As with the United States, its government is made up of three branches—the executive, the legislative, and the judicial.

THE EXECUTIVE BRANCH

Israel's head of state is the president. He or she is referred to by the title "nasi," which was the name for the head of the Sanhedrin, the legislative body of Israel in ancient times. The role of the president is mostly ceremonial. The president's duties include signing treaties and laws and opening the initial session of the Knesset, Israel's lawmaking body. But the

Israel's legislature meets in the Knesset building in Jerusalem, a historic structure that was completed in 1966. New wings were added in the 1990s and 2000s.

Prime Minister Netanyahu, *center*, consulted with several of his cabinet members following a vote at the Knesset in December 2018.

president does have some important powers. He or she is responsible for appointing judges and diplomats and, on the advice of the minister of justice, can pardon prisoners and commute prison sentences. Presidents are elected to one seven-year term by the members of the Knesset and are generally highly respected people known for their contributions to the state. There is no term limit for presidents.

As head of government, the prime minister is responsible for the day-to-day operations of the executive branch. This official is usually the leader of the political party with the most seats in the Knesset. One of the prime minister's most important responsibilities is choosing a member of the Knesset to draw up a list of candidates for the cabinet. Each candidate must then be approved by the entire Knesset.

Usually serving for four years, cabinet members, called ministers, are responsible for setting policy in a particular area of governance. For instance, there are ministers for finance, education, energy, justice, foreign affairs, health, tourism, and science and technology. Cabinet ministers are required to be citizens of Israel and must live in the country. They do not have to be members of the Knesset,

THE ISRAELI FLAG

The flag of Israel has a white field with a blue six-pointed star formed from two interlocking triangles. The symbol, known as the Star of David, became widely associated with Judaism in the 1800s. Above and below the Star of David are two horizonal blue bands inspired by the design of the tallit, a Jewish prayer shawl. The official color of the Star of David and the bands is sky blue, but flag makers interpret this in different ways. As a result, the hue seen on Israeli flags varies from light to dark blue.

MINI **BIO**

GOLDA MEIR

One of the most famous women of the 1900s, Golda Meir was the first woman to serve as the prime minister of Israel. She was born in Kyiv, Ukraine, in 1898 and moved with her family to the United States when she was eight. As an adult, she immigrated to Palestine, where she initially lived on a communal settlement called a kibbutz. Meir began working for Histadrut, Israel's major labor union, and became the head of its political division. After the creation of Israel in 1948, she traveled to the United States and raised $50 million from the American Jewish community to support the new state.[1]

In 1949, Meir was elected to the Knesset. Prime Minister David Ben-Gurion appointed her the Minister of Labor, then Foreign Minister. In 1966, she briefly retired before the Labor Party recruited her as prime minister in 1969. She served as Israel's leader until her resignation in 1974, after the Israeli military sustained heavy casualties in the Yom Kippur War with Egypt and Syria. Meir remained widely admired in Israel and abroad until her death in 1978 at age 80.

After Meir's death, the public learned that she had been battling leukemia for 12 years.

but they usually are. The entire cabinet meets once a week, although additional meetings are sometimes called to deal with pressing issues. If the prime minister cannot complete his or her term in office, the ministers appoint a cabinet member who is also in the Knesset to serve as the acting prime minister.

THE KNESSET

Israel's national lawmaking body, the Knesset, has one chamber of 120 members.[2] Its name and structure were inspired by the historical Kneset ha-Gedola, or great assembly, which was established in Jerusalem in the 400s BCE. Members of the Knesset are elected to four-year terms, but they often do not serve that long. The prime minister or the Knesset members themselves can choose to dissolve the body before its term is up and force a new election.

The Knesset is responsible for crafting policy and approving budgets, as well as passing laws. The body has 12 standing committees to deal with issues such as defense, finance, foreign affairs, education and culture, and the status of women. During each term, the Knesset can create special committees to oversee specific issues. Examples of

THE HOPE

In 2004, "Hatikvah" became the official anthem of Israel. The music was composed by Samuel Cohen, who based it on a Romanian folk song known as "The Ox-Driven Cart." The lyrics come from a poem written by Naftali Herz Imber in the 1870s. The anthem, whose title means "the hope," expresses the desire of the Jewish people: "To be a free nation in our land/ The Land of Zion and Jerusalem."[3]

Israelis still went to the polls in March 2021 during the COVID-19 pandemic.

special committees include ones dealing with the rights of children and with transparency and accessibility of government information. All debates in the Knesset are conducted in Hebrew, although its Arab members are also permitted to speak Arabic.

ELECTIONS AND POLITICAL PARTIES

Most Israelis are heavily engaged with their nation's politics. Usually between 77 percent and 87 percent of voters cast a ballot in elections for the Knesset.[4] At age 18, every Israeli citizen is eligible to vote, although candidates for the Knesset must be 21 or older. Election day is a holiday, and the government offers voters free transportation to the polls.

Israeli voters do not cast a ballot for specific candidates. They instead vote for a political party. Prior to the election, each party makes its platform public, along with a list of its Knesset candidates in order of the party's preference. The percentage of the vote received by each party determines how many of the 120 Knesset seats it takes. For instance, if a party receives 10 percent of the total vote, the first 12 people on its list of candidates will be elected, filling 10 percent of the Knesset.[5]

Israel has many political parties, including Likud, Labor, Yesh Atid, Shas, and Blue and White. Each Knesset includes representatives from ten to fifteen different parties.[6] Some parties are built around notable political personalities. One recent example was Kadima, which was dominated by former prime minister Ariel Sharon. Other parties represent people with particular religious identities or people of certain ethnicities, including parties for Israel's substantial Arab minority.

Traditionally, the two leading parties were Likud and Labor. Likud is relatively conservative, while Labor is considered moderate. But with the multiparty system, in which no single party can command a majority of Knesset seats, small parties often wield an outsize influence because the larger parties have to create coalitions in order to hold power. These coalitions are shaky and volatile, with parties often shifting their allegiances from one

JERUSALEM AS ISRAEL'S CAPITAL

Israel considers Jerusalem its capital. But much of the international community does not recognize it as such because Israel's 1968 annexation of East Jerusalem violated international law. The question of who controls Jerusalem is one of the reasons resolving the Israeli-Palestinian conflict is so difficult. The possibility of creating separate states for the Israelis and the Palestinians is complicated by the fact that both groups want to claim the holy city of Jerusalem as their capital.

group to another. This system has sometimes produced a dysfunctional government. For instance, in 2020 and 2021, Israel held four different elections in an effort to break a political stalemate that made the Knesset unable to pass a national budget for two years.[7]

THE JUDICIAL SYSTEM

According to the Basic Laws, the judicial branch of Israel is fully independent from the other two government branches. Judges are appointed by the president based on recommendations from a committee of legal experts. Judges serve until they are required to retire from the bench at age 70. Judges decide all cases. There is no trial by jury in Israel.

The Supreme Court, the highest court in Israel, hears appeals on rulings from lower courts. It also is often called on to determine whether laws passed by the Knesset conform to the principles set out in the Basic Laws. Magistrate and district courts hear civil and criminal cases. There are also specialized courts that deal with juvenile offenses, traffic violations, military offenses, and labor disputes. Disputes involving personal issues such as divorce, adoption, and guardianship are resolved by religious courts. Israel has separate religious courts for Jews, Muslims, Druze, and Christians.

LOCAL GOVERNMENT AND THE MILITARY

The country of Israel is divided into six administrative divisions called *mehozot*: Central, Haifa, Jerusalem, Northern, Southern, and Tel Aviv. These are further divided into 15 subdistricts.

Israel's Supreme Court is located near the Knesset in Jerusalem. Visitors can schedule tours of the building.

The minister of the interior appoints officials to oversee local governments within each district and subdistrict. Local governments are made up of elected councils of three types: municipal councils for large cities, local councils for smaller cities and towns, and regional councils for rural areas. These local governments are responsible for health services, schools, road and park maintenance, water supplies, fire protection, and collection of taxes.

Another part of the government that affects nearly all Israelis is the military. The IDF is one of the most well-trained militaries in the world. The IDF is also well funded, with military spending totaling about 5 percent of Israel's gross domestic product (GDP).[8] Hostilities with its Arab neighbors and terrorism in the occupied territories have compelled the nation to create and maintain a large and powerful military force.

The Israeli military employs about 173,000 people—130,000 in the ground forces, 34,000 in the air force, and 9,000 in the navy.[9]

The IDF is made up of an air force, a navy, and a small standing army, in addition to a large number of army reservists who can be called up to serve during times of war. At age 18, both men and women can be drafted. Men serve in the military for three years, and women serve for two. After their compulsory service is over, people may remain in the reserves until age 51.

Military service is required for all Jewish men and women and all Druze and Circassian men. Muslims and Christians can volunteer for some posts in the military. Most military jobs are open

Israel's powerful air force includes US-built F-35 stealth fighter jets.

to women, including those that involve combat. There are more than 3,000 women serving in combat units.[10] One group traditionally exempt from military service is the Haredi, ultra-Orthodox Jews who devote their lives to religious study. Recently, however, there has been significant pushback against this exemption by Israelis who feel the Haredi have a social and moral obligation to contribute to the national defense.

CHAPTER **SEVEN**

ECONOMICS

When Israel declared statehood in 1948, the new country faced many challenges. The most pressing was hostility with its Arab neighbors. But also critical was the need to improve its economy. At the time it became an independent nation, Israel was a small, relatively poor country with few natural resources and limited water for agriculture.

However, the unique circumstances of Israel's creation worked to bolster its economy in certain important ways. In its first decades, Israel received a large amount of capital from outside its borders. Wealthy Jewish people who wanted to support Israel poured money into the country. Israel also received grants from the United States government and war

The Jewish settlers who came to Israel in the 1940s, including farmers, faced hardship in the new country.

reparations from Germany. These funds helped finance the Israeli government's Development Budget, which was used to establish a manufacturing sector based initially on the production of food and textiles.

Israel's policy of encouraging Jews to immigrate led many well-educated Jews from Europe and North America to relocate. They brought with them skills and know-how in business and industry. Some also brought savings that contributed to the overall economy.

PLANNED TOWNS AND FARMING COOPERATIVES

In the country's early days, however, mass immigration also posed additional economic stresses. The country had to find ways to employ and house large numbers of new Israelis, many of whom had low levels of education. The government did not want new immigrants to cluster in large urban areas that could quickly become overcrowded. Instead it encouraged immigrants to live in new "development towns." These were dozens of planned rural settlements built mostly in Galilee and the Negev. Development towns were meant not only to quickly absorb immigrants but also to provide security to the state by populating largely empty territory.

Beersheba in northern Negev began as a development town. It has since become a significant city, the largest urban area in the Negev. But most development cities have not fared as well. Underfunded by the government, they have offered residents a limited number of manufacturing jobs. With many people forced into the low-paying seasonal labor market, isolated development towns are now among the poorest areas of the country.

Beersheba got its start as a home for newly arrived immigrants in the late 1940s.

Other economic experiments supported by the government included the development of kibbutzim and moshavim. A kibbutz is a planned rural settlement, usually devoted to agriculture but sometimes to a particular industry. The residents live communally and share the economic profits of their collective labor. The kibbutz provides shelter, food, clothing, medical care, and other necessities to everyone in the settlement. Any money left over is spent on improving the community. About 2 percent of Israelis live on kibbutzim.[1] A moshav is a group of family farms that works together in purchasing equipment and supplies and marketing their agricultural products. Today, there are about 450 moshavim operating in Israel.[2]

AGRICULTURE AND NATURAL RESOURCES

Israel's early leaders expected farming to play an important role in the economy. But today only 1 percent of the country's labor force works in agriculture.[3] Even so, thanks to mechanized farming, Israel is able to produce most of its own food supply. Israeli farmers grow a wide array of fruits and vegetables, including potatoes, tomatoes, carrots, turnips, peppers, tangerines, apples, grapes, and avocados. Animal products of Israel include beef, poultry, milk, and eggs.

The size of Israel's agricultural sector is limited by a lack of water needed for irrigation. In recent years, farmers have worked to increase their yields by making the most of irrigated lands. There are also efforts to increase the amount of water available by tapping water supplies beneath the desert in the Negev and by developing technology to desalinate seawater.

Israel also suffers from a lack of other natural resources, although its mining industry does produce materials needed for the manufacture of fertilizers, detergents, and pharmaceuticals. The Dead Sea is Israel's best source for minerals,

THE NEW ISRAELI SHEKEL

Israel's unit of currency is the new Israeli shekel (NIS). The currency's four colorful banknotes feature portraits of famous Hebrew poets who worked in the early and mid-1900s. The red 20 NIS note shows Rachel Bluwstein, better known as Rachel the Poetess, against a background of palm fronds. The green 50 NIS note depicts Shaul Tchernichovsky before a citrus tree. The profile of Leah Goldberg appears in front of almond tree blossoms on the orange 100 NIS note. And the blue 200 NIS note features Nathan Alterman against autumn leaves.

including potash, bromine, magnesium, and table salt. The Negev is also minerally rich, producing copper, clay, gypsum, and phosphates.

One important resource recently discovered by Israel is the natural gas found in the Tamar and Leviathan natural gas fields. These finds not only provide Israel with a secure supply of energy for domestic use but also give it a lucrative export good. In 2020, Israel began selling natural gas to Jordan and Egypt.

THE SERVICE AND INDUSTRIAL SECTORS

About 82 percent of Israel's labor force works in the service sector.[4] These jobs include work in retail, sales, marketing, finance, legal services, and many other fields. With its many religious and historical sites, Israel has a thriving tourism industry, employing large numbers of waiters, cooks, hotel staff, tour guides, and other

Israel's naturally dry climate can make agriculture challenging.

hospitality workers. The pleasant climate and excellent beaches along the Mediterranean Sea also attract vacationers. Most tourists in Israel are Europeans, although a substantial number come from North America.

Industry employs about 17 percent of the population.[5] The country's largest industrial centers are the cities of Tel Aviv and Haifa. Israel's manufactured products include machinery, plastics, pharmaceuticals, chemicals, processed foods, and textiles. In recent decades, Israel's industrial sector has seen its greatest growth in high-tech products, including electronics, computer systems, communication systems, and software. These are among Israel's leading export goods. Other exports include polished diamonds, medicines, medical instruments, and integrated circuits. Israel imports more goods than it exports. Imports include grains, raw materials, crude oil, and military equipment. The United States is Israel's most important trading partner, although Israel also does significant business with the European Union, the United Kingdom, China, India, and Hong Kong.

Israel's GDP was more than $394 billion in 2019.[6]

START-UP NATION

In the 2000s, Israel earned the nickname "start-up nation," a recognition that, per capita, it generates more high-tech start-up companies than any other country. As a center of high-tech innovation, it is second only to California's Silicon Valley. Israel's excellent university system in part explains this phenomenon. But experts believe the culture of the IDF also encourages entrepreneurs. Within the elite army intelligence units of the IDF, people are encouraged to take risks and think outside the box. These skills are useful for creating start-ups. The IDF also invests heavily in military technology that successful start-ups have been able to adapt for use in the private sector.

The high-tech boom is one of the greatest successes of Israel's economy. However, it has not benefited many of the country's laborers. Although people working in high-tech fields enjoy good salaries and high prestige, they account for only about 8 percent of the workforce.[7] Start-ups usually employ 30 people or less, most of whom are engineers. When an Israeli start-up is successful, it is rarely turned into a homegrown big business with hundreds of jobs for many kinds of workers, in part because Israel's workforce lacks the experienced managers needed to make that transition. When a start-up succeeds, its owners often instead sell it off to a multinational corporation.

DEALING IN DIAMONDS

Israel is a leading center for the trade and manufacturing of polished diamonds. The diamond industry operates out of the Israel Diamond Exchange, a complex of four high-rise buildings in the Tel Aviv area with a state-of-the-art security system. On its vast trading floor, buyers and sellers make deals for diamonds of every size, shape, and color. Deals are sealed with a handshake and the Hebrew words *mazal u'bracha*, meaning "may the deal be with luck and blessings."

ECONOMIC CHALLENGES

One of the most pressing economic challenges in Israel is wealth disparity. Many workers in manufacturing and service jobs are seeing their wages dropping, while the cost of housing, food, and consumer goods are high. About 22 percent of the Israeli population lives below the poverty line.[8] The government has developed policies to fight poverty, including minimum wage laws, child allowances, and income supplements. Still, income inequality remains a large and growing problem.

INNOVATIVE ISRAEL

Many ideas and inventions developed by Israeli high-tech start-ups have achieved success. One of the most popular is Waze, a GPS navigation app that gives directions to drivers on the best way to get to a destination, helping them avoid construction and traffic jams. Another is Watergen, a device that makes drinking water by pulling humidity out of the air. And a third is DayTwo, an app that analyzes the gut bacteria of people with diabetes to provide nutrition advice.

Another challenge for Israel's economy is its failing infrastructure. Critics contend that the government has not provided enough funds for building roads, while at the same time it has promoted car ownership. It also has invested very little in public transit. This has resulted in some of the worst traffic jams in the developed world. The amount of time workers spend in traffic hurts their productivity, costing the economy an estimated $10 billion a year.[9]

Israel's economic future is also threatened by the fact that the two segments of its population that are growing the fastest are also the most likely to be unemployed or underemployed—Arab Israelis and ultra-Orthodox Jewish Israelis. Arab Israelis have a separate school system, which critics

Israel's infrastructure challenges include severe traffic congestion on its roads. Traffic jams in large cities, such as Tel Aviv, are common.

say is underfunded. Students from the ultra-Orthodox community also have their own schools, where the instruction concentrates on religious studies. Students in these schools receive little training in mathematics, science, and other subjects needed to get good jobs. The problem of poverty and low workforce participation among Arab Israelis and ultra-Orthodox Israelis harms people in these groups. It is also likely to have a broad impact on the larger Israeli economy in the future because these groups taken together are estimated to become half of the total population in the coming decades.

ISRAEL TODAY

There is no single way to describe the daily life of an Israeli. After all, Israelis include high-tech professionals in Tel Aviv, Bedouin in desert encampments in the Negev, workers living communally in an agricultural kibbutz, and ultra-Orthodox families self-segregating in highly religious enclaves. Despite sharing a nationality, these groups' day-to-day experiences are extremely different from one another.

CITY LIFE

However, the vast majority of Israelis do have one thing in common. They are almost all urban dwellers.

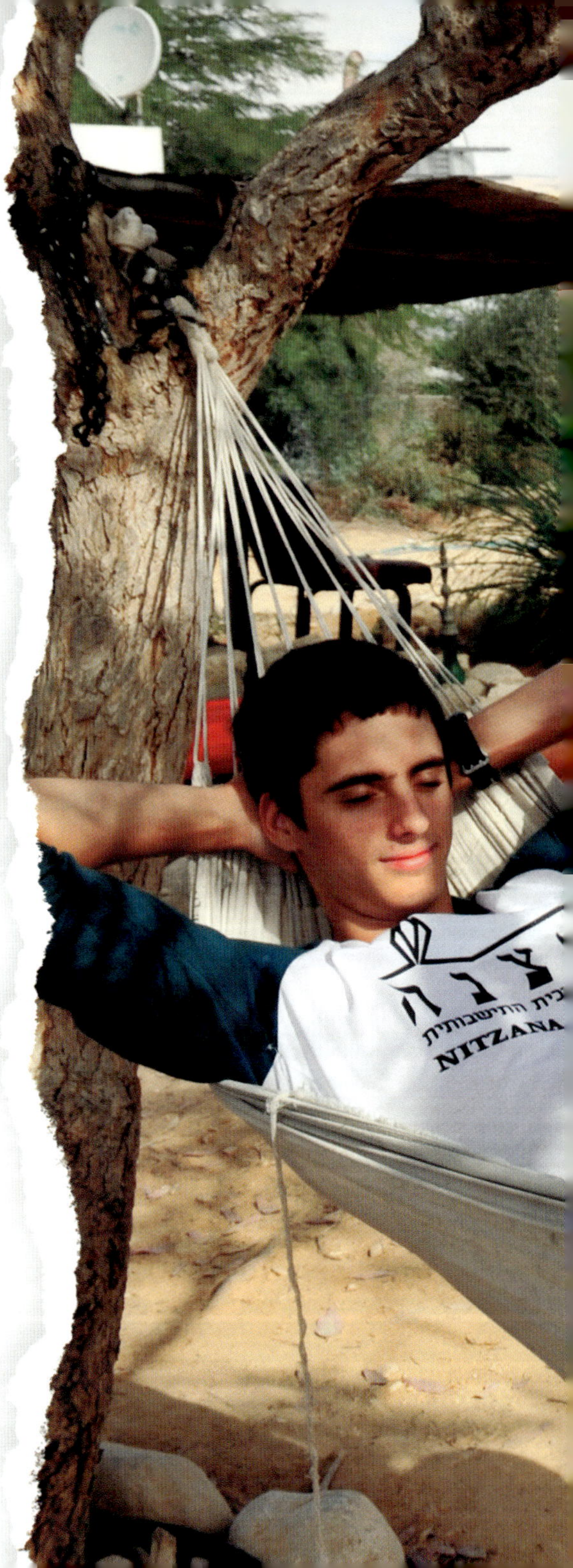

Daily life in Israel varies widely based on economic, geographical, and cultural factors. Life on a kibbutz may be significantly different from life in a big city or in a religious enclave.

About 93 percent of the population are residents of towns and cities.[1] About half of all Israelis live in the large coastal cities of Tel Aviv and Haifa.[2]

Most city dwellers live in apartments with two to four bedrooms and a large common area. They often have a small balcony where families gather to enjoy the evening breeze after a hot day. In smaller cities, apartment buildings are usually four to eight stories high, but in Tel Aviv many people live in high-rises because land there is very expensive. In Jerusalem, the height of new buildings is regulated in order to preserve the skyline. Laws going back to the Ottoman Empire require building facades to be constructed from Jerusalem stone, a local limestone that comes in white, cream, and soft pink hues.

SITTING SHIVA

Jewish families in Israel take great care in honoring elderly relatives after their deaths. Jewish law does not allow for cremation. Bodies instead must be buried after they are ritually cleansed and dressed in white cotton robes. The burial takes place as soon as possible, usually within 24 hours of death. Afterward, relatives sit shiva for seven days. During this mourning period, guests visit the relatives to talk about the deceased. On the annual anniversary of the death, relatives often visit the gravesite and light a long-burning candle in the deceased's honor.

FAMILY TIES

The focus of most Israelis' lives is their families. For secular Jews, the nuclear family includes about two children and their parents. More religiously observant parents often have larger families. Ultra-Orthodox women sometimes have as many as eight to twelve children.

Adults often live close to their parents and siblings, with everyone pitching in to help raise children. Children are given a great deal of attention, and parents work hard to ensure they will prosper in the future. In most families, both parents hold jobs outside the home. Within the ultra-Orthodox community, however, women are often the primary breadwinners so that their husbands can devote their time to religious scholarship. In more traditional families, the father is considered the head of the household, although mothers usually make decisions concerning the family. Younger parents, though, are more likely to share parenting and housekeeping duties.

The ties between parents and their adult children are often strong throughout their lives. They are likely to come together for the Jewish Shabbat dinner on Fridays and spend holidays and vacations together. When parents grow old, their children are expected to care for them.

DATING AND MARRIAGE

After graduating from high school, many Israelis go directly into the military. Once their service is over, they often spend the next few years going to college or starting a career. For most men and women, it makes sense to delay marriage until their mid- to late twenties.

To mark the coming of adulthood, Jewish families host bar mitzvah celebrations for boys at age 13 and bat mitzvah celebrations for girls at age 12.

Secular Israelis have male and female friends from an early age. They usually start dating in their

mid-teens. Encounters between young men and women are usually far more supervised among Muslims. In ultra-Orthodox Jewish communities, boys and girls are kept separate. When they reach marrying age, encounters with potential partners are organized by their parents and other relatives.

The Jewish wedding ceremony takes place under a canopy called a chuppah. It ends with the groom stepping on and breaking a glass, a symbol of the destruction of the two temples in ancient Jerusalem. After a wedding, both Jews and Muslims hold a lively celebration, where family and friends feast and dance.

SAME-SEX AND INTERFAITH MARRIAGES

Only religious wedding ceremonies can be held in Israel. Same-sex couples or couples of different faiths cannot be married in the country. Many such Israeli couples travel to the nearby island of Cyprus for their weddings. Unlike some of its Middle Eastern neighbors, Israel does officially recognize the marriages of same-sex and interfaith couples wed abroad.

CLOTHING

Most secular Jews and Arabs in Israel wear western clothing, like that worn in North America. Public dress for both men and women is fairly casual outside of formal settings. For example, people commonly wear shorts and sandals in the warm summer weather. Arab men often don a traditional headscarf called a keffiyeh, while Jewish men sometimes wear a circular yarmulke on their heads.

Ultra-Orthodox men often have sidelocks of hair called *payot* and wear black hats. They dress in long black coats over a shirt and pants. Ultra-Orthodox women wear clothing they consider modest. Their attire includes high-collared shirts, long skirts, and shoes with closed toes. Married Orthodox women may cover their hair with a wig called a sheitel. Many Muslim women also cover their head with a scarf called a hijab. The most religiously conservative wear a burka, a loose-fitting garment that completely covers the head and body.

LEISURE AND RECREATION

Israelis have many ways to enjoy their leisure time. In cities, there are plenty of movies, theater productions, and concerts to go to. People meet with friends and family at restaurants, bars, and clubs. Streetside cafés are a big part of many people's social lives. There, they spend hours chatting over coffee and treats. Older people often gather to play card games, backgammon, and chess.

Many Israelis are enthusiastic readers. In addition to Hebrew and Arabic literature, they can sample a wide array of local newspapers and periodicals. Most newspapers are in Hebrew, but papers in Arabic, English, Russian, Yiddish, German, Polish, French, Bulgarian, and Romanian are also available. Local television and radio programs are in Hebrew, Arabic, and English, but cable television also gives Israelis a good deal of international content. Israeli Arabs get much of their media from neighboring Arab countries.

Israelis love to explore the outdoors, so hiking, camping, and nature walks are popular, particularly in the spring and summer. On warm days, people crowd the beaches of Tel Aviv and

Elat to swim and sunbathe. For foreign travel, Turkey and Cyprus are popular destinations, while those who can afford it might take vacations in Europe.

SCHOOLS AND UNIVERSITIES

The Israeli people greatly value education. The government funds free schooling for all children through twelfth grade. The government allows students to choose between attending secular schools or religious schools, which provide religious scholarship and training as part of the curriculum. Schools for Jewish students are taught in Hebrew, while schools for Arab and Druze students are taught in Arabic. Starting in third grade, Hebrew-speaking children begin to study Arabic, and Arabic-speaking students are taught Hebrew. All students also have English classes.

Ultra-Orthodox students have their own independent schools. They concentrate on religious studies. After the early primary grades, girls and boys are taught separately.

Most young Israelis do not start college until after they have completed their military service,

MIZRAHI MUSIC

Throughout Israel, radios blast out an extremely popular genre of music known as Mizrahi. The songs blend musical traditions from Arab countries, such as Morocco, Iraq, and Yemen, while incorporating elements of blues, jazz, and Latin American and African music. Lyrics are often sung in both Hebrew and Arabic. Most Mizrahi artists are descendants of immigrants from countries in the Middle East and North Africa who arrived in Israel in the mid-1900s. The musical stew they create reflects their desire to combine their Arab heritage with their identity as modern Israelis.

so college freshmen are often older than 21. The majority of students in higher education go to colleges and universities in Israel. There are several major universities in the country, most notably the Hebrew University of Jerusalem, Tel Aviv University, and the University of Haifa. About 50 colleges are found throughout the country.[3]

KEEPING HEALTHY

Israelis have one of the highest life expectancies in the world. On average, they live to be 83 years old.[4] Everyone in the country can access health care through the state-run plan known as Kupat Holim. Many hospitals are public, but patients can go to private hospitals at an additional cost. National and local health-care authorities operate special medical facilities to provide health care for women of childbearing years. They care for mothers before and after a pregnancy and monitor the health of children during their first six years of life.

Israel's health-care system was tested in the 2020s with the onset of the COVID-19 pandemic. Early on, Israel's response was widely praised, especially when vaccines became available in December 2020. Within just three weeks, the country's aggressive vaccine rollout had vaccinated 20 percent of the eligible population. Israel's high rate of vaccination allowed the country to return largely to normal through much of 2021. Only when the highly contagious Omicron variant of the virus emerged late that year did Israel's caseload rise dramatically. At the height of the Omicron surge, Israel was seeing 100,000 cases a day, which severely stressed the country's overloaded hospital system.[5]

FUTURE CHALLENGES

Despite its advances in the high-tech industry, Israel still suffers from extreme income inequality and high rates of poverty. Although the government has worked to increase its fresh water supply, Israel will likely face severe water shortages in the years to come. Even though Israel has integrated many different groups into its society, there remain deep tensions within the Israeli population. These include tensions between the Jewish majority and the Arab minority, between secular Jews and ultra-Orthodox Jews, and between the Ashkenazi establishment and the Mizrahim on the rise.

Two of Israel's greatest problems are among its oldest: the conflict between Israelis and Arabs in the West Bank and the ongoing hostilities between Israel and neighboring Arab nations. The new coalition government formed in August 2021 offered some hope on both fronts. The government was the most politically and ethnically diverse in Israel's history. The coalition brought together politicians from both the right and left and was the first to include an Arab political party. For the first time in seven years, in 2021 a top Israeli minister met with Mahmoud Abbas, president of the Palestinian National Authority.

In March 2022, diplomats from Israel, the United States, and four Arab countries—Bahrain, Egypt, Morocco, and the United Arab Emirates—met in the Negev desert. It was the first Israeli-Arab diplomatic summit ever held on Israeli soil. No new policies emerged from the meeting, but photographs of the smiling diplomats suggested a real and growing cooperation between Israel and its neighbors that would have been unthinkable just a few decades ago. The participants committed to making the summit an annual event, perhaps drawing in other

Many people felt the March 2022 Negev Summit represented renewed hope for peace between Israel and its neighbors.

Arab nations. This prospect offered hope that a new era had begun that might someday bring lasting peace to the region.

ESSENTIAL **FACTS**

OFFICIAL NAME: MEDINAT YISRA'EL (STATE OF ISRAEL)

GEOGRAPHY

Area: 8,470 square miles (21,937 sq km)

Highest Elevation: Mitzpe Shlagim outpost at 7,297 feet (2,224 m)

Lowest Elevation: Dead Sea at –1,414 feet (–431 m)

PEOPLE

Population: 8.9 million (2022 est.)

Most Populous City: Tel Aviv–Yafo (4.3 million)

Ethnic Groups: Jewish, Arab, other

Religions: Judaism, Islam, Christianity, Druze, other

GOVERNMENT

Type of Government: Parliamentary democracy

Capital: Jerusalem (disputed by much of the international community)

Head of State: President

Head of Government: Prime minister

Legislature: Knesset

ECONOMY

Currency: New Israeli shekel

Major Industries: High-tech manufactured goods, wood and paper products, potash and phosphates, food, beverages

Natural Resources: Timber, potash, copper ore, natural gas, phosphate rock, magnesium bromide, clays, sand

NATIONAL SYMBOLS

National Anthem: "Hatikvah" ("The Hope")

National Bird: Hoopoe

National Flower: Anemone

GLOSSARY

ANTI-SEMITISM

Hostility toward or prejudice against Jews.

CARDAMOM

A spice made from an Indian herb.

DESALINATION

The process that removes salt and minerals from salty water.

ENTREPRENEUR

A person who organizes and operates a business or businesses.

EXODUS

The mass departure of a people from a geographical location.

GENOCIDE

Widespread, systematic acts of violence intended to destroy a national, ethnic, racial, or religious group.

GROSS DOMESTIC PRODUCT (GDP)

The monetary value of all final goods and services produced within a nation's geographic borders over a specified period of time.

HOMOGENEOUS
Made up of parts that are the same kind.

IRRIGATION
A system that brings water from one location to an area that has crops.

MILITANT
Aggressive in support of a political or social cause.

NATIONALIZE
To bring under the control of a country's government.

NONOBSERVANT
Declining to follow a rule, especially a religious custom or practice.

PARDON
To cancel the consequences of a legal offense.

SECULAR
Nonreligious.

SYNAGOGUE
The house of worship and communal center of a Jewish congregation.

ADDITIONAL **RESOURCES**

SELECTED BIBLIOGRAPHY

"Israel." *CIA World Factbook*, 2022, cia.gov. Accessed 28 Apr. 2022.

Israel and the Palestinian Territories. Lonely Planet, 2018.

Ochsenwald, William L., et al. "Israel." *Encyclopedia Britannica*, 2022, britannica.com. Accessed 28 Apr. 2022.

FURTHER READINGS

Buckey, A. W. *Egypt*. Abdo, 2023.

Jerusalem, Israel, and the Palestinian Territories. DK Eyewitness, 2019.

Lusted, Marcia Amidon. *The Israeli-Palestinian Conflict*. Abdo, 2018.

ONLINE RESOURCES

To learn more about Israel, please visit **abdobooklinks.com** or scan this QR code. These links are routinely monitored and updated to provide the most current information available.

MORE INFORMATION

For more information on this subject, contact or visit the following organizations:

The Embassy of Israel to the United States
3514 International Dr. NW
Washington, DC 20008
embassies.gov.il/washington/Pages/default.aspx
From this embassy in Washington, DC, Israel's ambassador oversees the country's diplomatic relationship with the United States.

The Israel Museum
11 Ruppin Blvd., Hakyria
Jerusalem, Israel
imj.org.il/en/collections
The Israel Museum features a vast array of art and archaeological objects. It is Israel's largest museum.

The Jewish Museum
1109 Fifth Ave.
New York, NY 10128
thejewishmuseum.org
The Jewish Museum maintains a collection of about 30,000 works of art and ceremonial objects relating to Jewish life around the world.

SOURCE **NOTES**

CHAPTER 1. A TOUR OF ISRAEL

1. "Dome of the Rock." *Encyclopedia Britannica*, 25 Apr. 2022, britannica.com. Accessed 6 July 2022.
2. "Population of Israel and Jerusalem." *Jerusalem Institute*, 2020, jerusaleminsitute.org.il. Accessed 6 July 2022.
3. "The Model of Jerusalem in the Second Temple Period." *Israel Museum*, 2022, imj.org.il. Accessed 6 July 2022.
4. "Hezekiah's Tunnels, City of David." *iTravelJerusalem*, n.d., itraveljerusalem.com. Accessed 6 July 2022.
5. "What Was the Holocaust?" *Yad Vashem*, 2022, yadvashem.org. Accessed 6 July 2022.

CHAPTER 2. GEOGRAPHY

1. "Israel." *CIA World Factbook*, June 24, 2022, cia.gov. Accessed 6 July 2022.
2. William L. Ochsenwald et al. "Israel." *Encyclopedia Britannica*, 6 July 2022, britannica.com. Accessed 6 July 2022.
3. "Geography and Climate." *Israel Ministry of Foreign Affairs*, 4 Nov. 2021, gov.il. Accessed 6 July 2022.
4. Ochsenwald et al., "Israel," *Encyclopedia Britannica*.
5. "Geography and Climate," *Israel Ministry of Foreign Affairs*.
6. Ochsenwald et al., "Israel," *Encyclopedia Britannica*.
7. "Israel," *CIA World Factbook*.
8. "Geography and Climate," *Israel Ministry of Foreign Affairs*.
9. Ochsenwald et al., "Israel," *Encyclopedia Britannica*.
10. "Geography and Climate," *Israel Ministry of Foreign Affairs*.
11. "Geography and Climate," *Israel Ministry of Foreign Affairs*.
12. "Israel," *CIA World Factbook*.
13. Nir Hasson. "Tehran Caves to Israel: World's Largest Salt Cavern Discovered, Beating Iranian Record." *Haaretz*, 28 Mar. 2019, haaretz.com. Accessed 6 July 2022.
14. "Israel." *World Book*, 2022, worldbookonline.com. Accessed 6 July 2022.
15. Ochsenwald et al., "Israel," *Encyclopedia Britannica*.
16. Abigail Klein Leichman. "Dead Sea Is Shrinking but It's Not Exactly Dying." *Jewish Star*, 20 Oct. 2021, thejewishstar.com. Accessed 6 July 2022.
17. Seth M. Siegel. "How to Defeat Drought: Lessons from Israel's War for Water." *Foreign Policy*, Apr. 2018, foreignpolicy.com. Accessed 6 July 2022.

CHAPTER 3. PLANTS AND ANIMALS

1. "Flora and Fauna in Israel." *Israel Ministry of Foreign Affairs*, 2022, mfa.gov.il. Accessed 6 July 2022.
2. "Israel." *CIA World Factbook*, June 24, 2022, cia.gov. Accessed 6 July 2022.
3. "Flora and Fauna in Israel," *Israel Ministry of Foreign Affairs*.
4. Daniel Estrin. "A PSA Campaign Got Israelis to Stop Picking Flowers in Order to Preserve Them." *World*, 18 Jan. 2016, theworld.org. Accessed 6 July 2022.
5. "Indian Porcupine." *Animalia*, n.d., animalia.bio. Accessed 6 July 2022.
6. William L. Ochsenwald et al. "Israel." *Encyclopedia Britannica*, 6 July 2022, britannica.com. Accessed 6 July 2022.
7. "Flora and Fauna in Israel," *Israel Ministry of Foreign Affairs*.
8. "Flora and Fauna in Israel," *Israel Ministry of Foreign Affairs*.
9. Aaron Reich. "Thousands of Cranes Flock to Israel's North as Migration Season Begins." *Jerusalem Post*, 14 Oct. 2021, jpost.com. Accessed 6 July 2022.
10. Ori Lewis and Naama Shilony. "Bats Occupy Israeli Army Ghost Bunkers." *Reuters*, 27 Jan. 2012, reuters.com. Accessed 6 July 2022.

CHAPTER 4. HISTORY

1. William L. Ochsenwald et al. "Israel." *Encyclopedia Britannica*, 6 July 2022, britannica.com. Accessed 6 July 2022.
2. Ochsenwald et al., "Israel," *Encyclopedia Britannica*.
3. Ochsenwald et al., "Israel," *Encyclopedia Britannica*.
4. "Israel Profile – Timeline." *BBC News*, 9 Apr. 2019, bbc.com. Accessed 6 July 2022.
5. "The Law of Return." *The Jewish Agency for Israel*, n.d., jewishagency.org. Accessed 6 July 2022.
6. "Israel Profile – Timeline," *BBC News*.
7. "Israel Profile – Timeline," *BBC News*.

CHAPTER 5. PEOPLE AND CULTURE

1. William L. Ochsenwald et al. "Israel." *Encyclopedia Britannica*, 6 July 2022, britannica.com. Accessed 6 July 2022.
2. Yossi Mekelberg. "The Plight of Ethiopian Jews in Israel." *BBC News*, 25 May 2015, bbc.com. Accessed 6 July 2022.
3. Eileen Lavine. "Proud and Prickly with a Soft Heart." *Moment*, 2012, momentmag.com. Accessed 6 July 2022.
4. "Israelis." *Worldmark Encyclopedia of Cultures and Daily Life*, 2017, gale.com. Accessed 6 July 2022.
5. "Jewish Population Rises to 15.2 Million Worldwide." *Jewish Agency for Israel*, 5 Sept. 2021, jewishagency.org. Accessed 6 July 2022.

SOURCE **NOTES** CONTINUED

6. "Israel." *CIA World Factbook*, June 24, 2022, cia.gov. Accessed 6 July 2022.
7. "The People." *CultureGrams*, 2021, online.culturegrams.com. Accessed 6 July 2022.
8. Oren Kessler. "Circassians Are Israel's Other Muslims." *Forward*, 20 Aug. 2012, forward.com. Accessed 6 July 2022.
9. Gabe Friedman. "Could Gal Gadot Become the Biggest Israeli Superstar Ever?" *Times of Israel*, 26 May 2017, timesofisrael.com. Accessed 6 July 2022.
10. Marlow Stern. "Gal Gadot's Wonder Woman: A Hamas-Bashing, Ex-IDF Soldier and Former Miss Israel." *Daily Beast*, 14 Apr. 2017, thedailybeast.com. Accessed 6 July 2022.
11. "Maccabi Playtika Tel Aviv." *EuroLeague Basketball*, n.d., euroleaguebasketball.net. Accessed 6 July 2022.
12. "2021 Maccabiah Games Postponed by a Year amid Coronavirus Pandemic." *Times of Israel*, 2 Apr. 2022, timesofisrael.com. Accessed 6 July 2022.

CHAPTER 6. POLITICS

1. Letty Cottin Pogrebin. "Golda Meir." *Jewish Women's Archive*, n.d., jwa.org. Accessed 6 July 2022.
2. "Political Structure and Elections." *Israel Ministry of Foreign Affairs*, 2022, mfa.gov.il. Accessed 6 July 2022.
3. "National Anthem." *Knesset*, n.d., knesset.gov.il. Accessed 6 July 2022.
4. "Political Structure and Elections," *Israel Ministry of Foreign Affairs*.
5. "Political Structure and Elections," *Israel Ministry of Foreign Affairs*.
6. "Political Structure and Elections," *Israel Ministry of Foreign Affairs*.
7. Patrick Kingsley. "As 4th Election Looms, Some Ask: Is Israel's Democracy Broken?" *New York Times*, 24 Mar. 2021, nytimes.com. Accessed 6 July 2022.
8. "Israel." *CIA World Factbook*, June 24, 2022, cia.gov. Accessed 6 July 2022.
9. "Israel," *CIA World Factbook*.
10. "Israel," *CIA World Factbook*.

CHAPTER 7. ECONOMICS

1. "Israelis." *Worldmark Encyclopedia of Cultures and Daily Life*, 2017, gale.com. Accessed 6 July 2022.
2. "Israelis," *Worldmark Encyclopedia*.
3. "Israel." *CIA World Factbook*, June 24, 2022, cia.gov. Accessed 6 July 2022.
4. "Israel," *CIA World Factbook*.
5. "Israel," *CIA World Factbook*.
6. "Israel," *CIA World Factbook*.
7. Shoshanna Solomon. "Vaunted High-Tech Sector Not Solution to Israel's Economic Problems, Book Says." *Times of Israel*, 21 June 2018, timesofisrael.com. Accessed 6 July 2022.
8. "Israel," *CIA World Factbook*.
9. David M. Halbfinger and Isabel Kershner. "Israel, 'Start-up Nation,' Groans under Strains of Growth and Neglect." *New York Times*, 1 Mar. 2020, nytimes.com. Accessed 6 July 2022.

CHAPTER 8. ISRAEL TODAY

1. "Israel." *CIA World Factbook*, June 24, 2022, cia.gov. Accessed 6 July 2022.
2. William L. Ochsenwald et al. "Israel." *Encyclopedia Britannica*, 6 July 2022, britannica.com. Accessed 6 July 2022.
3. "The People." *CultureGrams*, 2021, online.culturegrams.com. Accessed 6 July 2022.
4. "Israel," *CIA World Factbook*.
5. Eric Reguly. "Israel Having Trouble Repeating Its World-Leading Success in Fighting the Pandemic as Omicron Cases Surge." *Globe and Mail*, 3 Feb. 2022, theglobeandmail.com. Accessed 6 July 2022.

INDEX

ABOUT THE **AUTHOR**

LIZ SONNEBORN

A graduate of Swarthmore College, Liz Sonneborn has written more than 100 books for young readers and adults on a wide variety of subjects. Her specialties include American history, world history, biography, women's studies, and African American studies. She is the author of more than a dozen books about the history and culture of various countries, including Mexico, Canada, France, Iraq, Yemen, Kuwait, and Haiti.